POWER OUTAGE

Mike Larrimore Brian Pivik
Bill Yon

POWER OUTAGE

CONTRIBUTORS

WRITTEN AND DEVELOPED BY:

Mike Larrimore, Brian Pivik, & Bill Yon

EDITOR:

Brian Pivik

PROOFREADING:

Alexandra James

ART DIRECTION AND LAYOUT:

Sophia Conner

COVER AND INTERNAL ART:

James Alexander

CARTOGRAPHY:

Sophia Conner

PROJECT MANAGEMENT:

Lawrence Whitaker

PLAYTESTERS:

Steve Burk, Rob Colondo, David Cunningham, Pat Lenz, Chuck McGinnis, & Bill Yon

We dedicate this book to the memory of Rob Colondo. You are on a grand adventure dear friend, and in your absence we shall tell tales of your glory.

Power Outage © 2024 by The Design Mechanism

Mythras is a Registered Trademark ® of The Design Mechanism. All rights reserved. This edition of *Power Outage* is copyright © 2023. This book may not be reproduced in whole or in part by any means without permission from The Design Mechanism, except as quoted for purposes of illustration, discussion and game play. Reproduction of the material in this book for the purposes of personal or corporate profit, by photographic, electronic, or other methods of retrieval is strictly prohibited.

FIND US AT:

www.thedesignmechanism.com and www.mythrasrpg.com.

Facebook: https://www.facebook.com/The-Design-Mechanism
MeWe: https://mewe.com/join/the_design_mechanism
Twitter#designmech
Podcast: https://www.buzzsprout.com/266482

CONTENTS

Adventure Outline	4
Missing Pieces	5
Down the Tubes	7
Into the Woods	10
Welcome to Gemelos	13
Inconvenient Convenience	16
The Doctor is In	19
Revelations	24
Antagonists and Allies	27
Appendix	31
Maps and Plans	35

POWER OUTAGE

Trapped! Waking up inside a fluid filled glass tube, there is little time to get free and take stock before mysterious and malevolent robots descend on you, intent on stopping you at whatever cost. Whoever their master is wants you back as an unwilling test subject; and stuck in the middle of the woods, you have few options for escape. If your situation wasn't bad enough, you awoke with mere fragments of memories of who you are, and stranger yet, you keep manifesting strange and fantastic powers when under duress. Even if you make it back to civilization you still need to shake your automated pursuers while you try to figure out why this is all happening to you. Will you find the answers in Gemelos City, or will you spend the rest of your life as a science project for a mysterious villain?

Welcome to *Power Outage*, a scenario for *Destined* (you will need this book to make the most of Power Outage). In this adventure your players take on the roles of seemingly normal people caught in a bizarre situation, made weirder by the strange extranormal abilities that manifest when they are under duress. Over the course of the adventure, Heroes will unlock an array of special Core Powers, but they are also affected by an experimental drug that causes these new-found abilities to falter when least expected. This adventure can serve as an introduction to *Destined* for new or veteran players alike, but it can also be inserted into an existing campaign, and guidelines are provided on how to use it with established Heroes. While designed for Heroes of the Epic Power Level, guidelines are given to adjust them for Street and Paragon Level Heroes.

Adventure Outline

1. The Heroes awaken from a drug-induced coma, trapped inside human-sized fluid filled glass tubes.

• The Heroes have near total amnesia regarding who they are and that they possess powers.

• The Heroes must find a way out of the tubes before they drown.

2. The Heroes discover they were being transported in an automated truck that overturned while on a dirt road deep in the woods.

• The Heroes must quickly get their bearings and examine the scene for clues, before encountering a group of aggressive flying robots approaching the scene.

• The villain dispatched these drones to investigate why the delivery truck had not arrived on schedule.

- Whether the Heroes fight or flee the robots, the stress of the situation begins to jog their memory.

2.1. The Heroes discover one of their Core Powers.

2.2. The Heroes regain their highest ranked Passion.

3. The Heroes need to decide where to go next, but eventually they find themselves on the outskirts of Gemelos City in the suburbs of the Crown.

- The robots continue to hound them.

- With each stressful encounter, the Heroes manifest another Core Power (up to their normal amount based on Power Level), and regain more of their memories.

4. During their explorations the Heroes encounter a few potential allies.

- Callie Carter – an investigative journalist/conspiracy theorist who was working with one of the Heroes prior to their capture. Callie is a friendly NPC who will try to help the heroes recover their memories and their powers, and she is aware of Dr. Julian's work but unaware of his true nature. As the Games Master, be sure that you're well-informed of Callie and her motives.

- Dr. Carl Julian – a physician and geneticist, online contact of Callie.

5. Dr. Julian offers to try to help them regain all their memories and Core Powers if they accompany him to his lab.

- Dr. Julian interviews and performs tests on the Heroes.

- The Heroes may notice that Dr. Julian is not being honest about his motivations.

6. The Heroes discover that Dr. Julian is secretly the developer of a drug designed to impair the use of extranormal powers, the same drug that was administered to the Heroes prior to them waking up.

- Dr. Julian attempts to kill the Heroes, either through trickery or openly, forcing the Heroes to defend themselves.

> ## C.O.P. ALERTS
>
> If you would like to expand the adventure, or add in additional encounters, included C.O.P. Alerts in the scenario offer optional side encounters that can be inserted or used as inspiration for your own additions. Note that any Non-Player Characters listed in C.O.P. Alerts are not detailed and the Games Master should flesh them out if they would like them to have a greater role in the scenario.

- The Heroes learn that an unknown villain funded Dr. Julian's research.

MISSING PIECES

The Heroes are stripped of their memories and Core Powers at the beginning of the adventure, a side effect of the drug that was administered to them. The drug is designed to prevent extranormal Heroes from accessing their powers by putting blocks on the parts of the brain that control their abilities, but it is not as effective as the villain, Praxagore, believed, and its effects are countered by surges of cortisol and adrenaline during stressful situations. Over the course of the adventure the Heroes regain what they lost, and if you are using this adventure as the starting-off point of a series of *Destined* adventures, you can also use this as part of the creation process (if you and your group choose to do so). Below are a few suggestions about how to incorporate the Heroes regaining their faculties as part of group character creation.

- **Pre-Made Heroes**: The Heroes are created prior to the start of the adventure, using a Power Level determined by the group and completing all steps as outlined in Chapter 1 of the *Destined* core rulebook. At the start of the adventure, the Heroes do not have access to any of their Core Powers or Passions, regaining access to them as outlined below. The Heroes have access to their normal Skills, but they cannot recall who they are, including their name and any background details of their life prior to waking up. Since the Heroes already have established Passions, whenever a situation comes up where a hero's choice might contradict one of their Passions, the Games Master rolls against the forgotten Passion, and if successful the hero is not able to act as they planned, but is not sure why until the Passion is regained.

- **Creation During Play**: If you choose you can also develop the Heroes during the course of the adventure. Before the session starts, all players should complete steps 1 through 9 of the character creation process based on the chosen Power Level, having their Characteristics, Attributes, and Skills completed. When they regain a Power or Passion during the adventure, the players can choose them at that time, also adding any Boosts and Limits for the Core Power as allowed by their Power Level. To prevent delays in play, the Games Master can have players go through the Core Powers list to note any they are interested in and think about personality traits of their Heroes to help define their Passions. Alternatively, if the players permit it, the Games Master can choose the first Power and/or Passion each hero gains and the players can build from that as the adventure progresses.

- **Skills During Play**: If your players want to start off as blank slates, you can also have them make decisions about their trained Skills during the adventure. With this option it is recommended you use the Quick Hero Creation rules found on page 50 of the *Destined* core rulebook. Players create their Heroes as normal, assigning Characteristics and calculating their Attributes and the base values of their Standard Skills. Whenever they need to use a Standard Skill, they can choose to assign one of the skill modifiers for their Power Level. If a Professional Skill is required, a hero can choose to gain that Skill and add one of their skill modifiers, up to a maximum of seven Professional Skills. When the Heroes regain the last of their three Passions and have their memories restored (see page 23), they can assign any remaining skill modifiers as their full memory is restored.

- **Random Creation**: For some old school superhero roleplaying fun, players can also choose to generate their Core Powers randomly using the table located on page 31 of this adventure. This can be done prior to the start of the adventure or whenever the hero regains a power. Note that random generation of Core Powers can lead to some strange combinations, so the Games Master can allow players to roll twice and choose the power that appeals to them. There is also a table of random example Passions located on page 33. This can be used to generate a Passion whenever the Heroes regain one, or as an aid for players who are having trouble producing Passions for their Heroes.

IMPAIRED ORIGINS

Praxagore's drug treatment is designed for people who are affected by the Godstrand, a genetic abnormality that causes the manifestation of powers. The Godstrand is tied to most Origins listed in the core rulebook, but Heroes with Mystical, Technology, and Training Origins would not normally be affected by it, since their powers come from non-biological sources. The simplest solution for the Games Master is to say the mental blocks caused by the drug also impair the hero's ability to recall having powers, preventing them from accessing special abilities and Skills. If a hero's Core Powers come from an External Power Source, such as a magical amulet or a suit of powered armor, that item should be present in the truck at the start of the adventure inside a storage locker. The hero either regains all the powers normally granted by the item when they put it on or the mental blocks prevent them from accessing all their powers. As they regain their abilities, they also remember how to utilize everything the object can do. Perhaps the hero can use the Core Powers granted by the object, but not as effectively until they fully regain their memories, suffering a penalty to any Skill checks required for the Core Powers until they restore all their Passions.

For example, Pentacle the sorceress and Steel Sovereign both have Core Powers granted by External Power Sources (a mystical bracelet and a suit of powered armor respectively). The Games Master decides Pentacle is unable to recall how her bracelet works at the start of the adventure, and Steel Sovereign can don his armor but can only access the Inherent Armor and Enhanced Strength Core Powers at the start but he has poor control. Pentacle would regain her powers as outlined, and Steel Sovereign would make any Brawn, Combat Style, or Unarmed Skill checks at one Difficulty Grade harder until his memories are restored.

If the hero has the Artificial Being power the Games Master should modify some details of the adventure to account for the hero's nature as a non-biological being. Perhaps the power suppressant medication would not work on them, but Dr. Julian conducted experiments on them to learn of their nature as a way of developing the means to cancel out their Core Powers as well. While his experiments did not inflict any lasting harm, they have caused some of the hero's abilities

The Heroes awaken in the wreckage of a crashed truck not knowing who they are, or how they got there.

to malfunction temporarily. These Heroes were rendered inert by his experiments and they awaken in tubes just like their compatriots, and they awake with all their normal Core Powers but no memories until they regain all their Passions as detailed in the adventure. They also suffer from the Power Outage Limit as detailed below until they regain all their memories.

Using Pre-Existing Characters

If you are using this adventure as part of an ongoing *Destined* storyline, there are a few modifications you so can still use the plot as written with established Heroes. Using pre-existing Heroes is handled much like using Pre-Made Heroes as detailed above, but since the players have more of a history with their characters this creates an exercise in good roleplaying, as they need to act like they know nothing about their hero.

Down the Tubes

The adventure starts with the Heroes waking up inside glass tubes filled with an amber-colored solution. The tubes are attached to racks on the ceiling of the inside of an AI-driven truck. The tubes were being transported through the far edge of the Pholos State Park outside Gemelos City. The AI malfunctioned and the truck drove off the road into a gully, hitting a tree head on. When this occurred, the machinery maintaining the equipment that kept the Heroes in stasis was disabled, and they immediately snapped out of their drug-induced slumber. Read the following:

Power Outage

> *Your eyes snap open and immediately begin to sting, a dull burn from the liquid you are submerged in, and you can just make out faint light in some darkened chamber. Panic sets in, raw and primal, and as your hands and feet snap out, they hit what feels like glass. As you feel around there is glass all around you, metal above you, and your arms get tangled in tubing attached to a mask covering the lower half of your face. Your breathing is ragged and panicked, made more so when you realize the mask is not providing you any breathable air. You are trapped in a glass tube in a darkened room, moments away from asphyxiating. Somewhere around you there are dull, muted thuds. Are you the only one in a tube or are there others waking up to the same fate? What do you do?*

At this point, the Heroes do not have access to any Core Powers, and they need to rely on their natural Characteristics and Skills to extract themselves from the tubes. The failing life support systems only have a few (1d3+1) turns of oxygen left before the Heroes risk Asphyxiation. The 'glass' is a thin, clear polycarbonate material with 1 Armor Point and 4 Hit Points. The Heroes have enough room to strike it with their fists or feet using an Easy Unarmed check, or inflicting their standard damage with a successful Unarmed check. Once the material's Hit Points are depleted, it cracks and the pressure of the fluid rushing out opens up enough of the tube for the hero to escape. Heroes trained in Electronics or Mechanisms can also attempt to find a way to trigger a release at the top of the tube's interior, causing the bottom to swing open. If a hero is having difficulty escaping the other Heroes can assist in getting them free, or the Games Master can have them make a check with the higher of their Endurance or Willpower Skills. If successful, the hero manifests one of their Core Powers early, using the guidelines listed in the next encounter. The power lasts long enough to aid in their escape but fades immediately afterwards, manifesting fully as detailed below.

Once they are out of the tubes, the Heroes have only a few minutes to examine the situation and get their bearings. They are all dressed in matching one-piece white unitards, and the fluid they were immersed in leaves a medicinal smell on them until it is washed off. They have no memory of their lives before that moment, specifically personal details including their names, family members, or their life histories. Unless using the *Skills During Play* creation option above, they also retain knowledge of inherent or learned Skills, although they can't recall how they acquired that knowledge. The interior of the truck is spartan, containing only several small storage lockers mounted to the wall on the opposite side of the cab, and inside the lockers are any power-related equipment the Heroes would normally have, a small emergency first aid kit with basic supplies, and a small mechanics tool kit that includes a tire iron that can be used as a baton in combat (see *Destined*, page 130). If the Heroes take some time to search the truck and the immediate area, they can learn the following by simple observation:

- The tubes they were held in are very high-tech, and they were hooked up to a ceiling-mounted medical monitoring system. The system is currently non-functional due to the crash, which damaged the truck's power systems. With a successful Electronics or Mechanics check, the monitoring system can be opened up and examined. There are three oxygen tanks installed and the system itself was designed to monitor the vitals of the Heroes and keep the temperature inside the tubes regulated. There is an installed

First Power and Passion

The stress of encountering the drones and the knowledge they are a threat causes a surge of adrenaline in the Heroes that counteracts the drug that is suppressing their abilities. This causes one of their lost Core Powers to emerge and a surge of lost memories represented by regaining one of their Passions. At this time, the hero may choose one Core Power of their choice as determined by the method of creation as outlined above. The power has any Boosts and Limits already assigned to it, or the player may assign them at this time as detailed above. They also regain their highest valued Passion and recall either their actual name or the name they used when operating as a hero (player's choice). The hero still does not recall many details of their former life, but the Games Master may allow the player to give one event from their former life or roll on one of the Background Event tables from the core rulebook to flesh out some part of the hero's backstory.

memory card within the system that can be ejected, and if the Heroes find a way to access the data later down the road, it shows a record of all their vital signs over the course of three days. There is no identifying information for the Heroes, with each one being referred to by a number, and the only thing noted within the data is the word "praxagore" in the main file name.

• The truck appears to be a large, four-wheeled refrigeration truck on the outside. It has no distinct markings such as company logos or identification numbers, and it has a California commercial license plate on the back. If the Heroes try to trace the license plate sometime later, it is registered to a dummy company called Praxagore Consulting. The front cab is almost completely crushed, a large limb of the tree it crashed into smashing down the roof of the cab. The truck is all electric and what is left of the engine is still sparking. If the Heroes try to gain access to the cab, they can briefly see a flickering hologram of a uniformed driver before the system fails and it disappears. A successful Computers or Electronics check identifies some of the visible components as an advanced automated driving system, although it is far too damaged to get any information out of the memory or the destroyed GPS system.

• The Heroes are in the middle of an old growth forest with large redwood trees and thick patches of ferns as a majority of the groundcover. The truck is down in a small gully and the Heroes can easily trace the path it took through the disrupted dirt and underbrush from the dirt road that lies just up a small hill. The Heroes can also determine the direction the truck was headed before it veered off, although there is no obvious cause for the crash. A successful Easy Navigation (Forest) or Survival check helps the Heroes get their bearings enough to know from the moon that it's before midnight, the truck was traveling from west to east, and this type of forest reinforces that they are most likely somewhere in California. During the few minutes they have before the next encounter, the Heroes can also forage for some stout tree limbs to use as makeshift batons or clubs if they feel the need to arm themselves.

Celedrones, flying robot minions of the villain Praxagore, are already in the woods, hunting for the Heroes.

During the brief time they have to explore the area, the Heroes also have the opportunity to get to know each other, although with their memory loss there is not much to share. If the Heroes examine their own bodies they can find distinguishing features such as tattoos and scars if the Heroes wish to add those features, but with a Hard First Aid or Medicine check they also locate a recent scar on each of their underarms just below their armpits. This marks a sub-dermal GPS tracking chip inserted into the Heroes, and this allows their kidnappers to locate the Heroes wherever they are. As long as the chips remain intact, any Track checks made by the antagonists are one Difficulty Grade easier. Given the time and tools (and the willingness to take 1 Hit Point of damage to the arm in question), Heroes can make a Hard First Aid or Normal Medicine check to remove a single chip. If examined, the tracking chips have no identifying markers.

After the Heroes have had a short while to explore their surroundings, or if they follow the truck's path of carnage back to the road, move on to the next encounter.

INTO THE WOODS

When the truck malfunctioned and crashed, it sent out a brief emergency signal to its owners, informing them that one of its systems failed. The signal ended when it impacted the tree, but it lasted long enough to provide a generalized last location before its systems went completely offline. The owners dispatched a squad of Celedrones (see page 27) to its last known location to determine what happened to the truck. There are two Celedrones plus one more for each hero, and they move fast enough in flight to arrive at the site within a few minutes of the Heroes waking up. After the Heroes have had a short amount of time to explore their immediate surroundings, read the following:

> *Just when you were starting to get accustomed to the darkness and sounds of the woods, everything around you suddenly becomes deathly quiet. The sounds of crickets and the dull creak of tree limbs are replaced with a distant hum from up in the sky. Too fast for your liking, the sound grows closer, never rising above a low whirl, and no more than a few hundred meters away a single red spotlight appears. It emanates from somewhere just below the treetops, scanning the ground below in slow sweeps. Then another appears, and another... More and more lights snap on, each one scanning a different section of the forest floor in a gentle cadence. You watch for a moment, at first out of curiosity, but that quickly turns into primal panic when you notice the sweeping red lights are steadily moving forwards in your direction.*

The Celedrones begin slowly scanning the area, looking for the truck but also following the signals produced by the tracking implants in each hero's arm. They spread out, but remain within 100 meters of each other so they can do a focused search, and one moves to the dirt road to search there. The drones move at half their normal Flight Movement Rate while searching, but their scanning lights reach out to 50 meters away, moving back and forth in a steady pace until it finds something of interest. The drones also have audio sensors that extend out to 100 meters away. If the drones get within that range of any of the Heroes, the Celedrones can make a Perception check, modified by any cover the Heroes have or opposed by their Stealth checks. They may also make Perception checks if the Heroes make any noise or do something that would draw their attention. Once a hero is located, all drones alert and they converge on that location. If the drones locate the truck before the Heroes, two of them go to the site while the remainder continue scanning the woods.

Whether the Heroes are still by the truck, on the road, or they moved out into the woods, they remain within the search radius of the Celedrones if they don't take action. If the Heroes need motivation they observe one of the drones lock onto a red fox and it immediately fires out a barrage of projectiles. The Heroes are able to see a crackle of electricity whenever the projectiles hit, including the poor hapless animal. This may also dissuade them from approaching the drones and help them determine the machines are a threat.

While the Heroes are free to choose whatever course of action they like, there are a few immediate options for them.

- **They can run away**. The Heroes can try to escape the drones by running down the road or deeper into the woods. The woods provide move cover for their escape, but the road does hold the promise of eventually leading back to civilization. This is treated as an Extended Task (see *Destined*, page 57), with the Heroes using their Athletics (if using the road) or Stealth (if using the woods) Skills against the Perception Skills of the drones. If the Heroes remain together as they flee this will be treated as a group Extended Task for them. They are detected if the drones reach 100% before they do, and the drones converge on their location. Unless the Heroes successfully hide or distract the drones, a combat encounter begins. If the Heroes accumulate enough successes to reach 100% before the drones do, they can get far enough away from the machines to reach outside their search path.

- **They can fight**. The Heroes can try to attack the drones and disable or destroy them. As mentioned above they can use tree branches as makeshift weapons, and they can also throw rocks or create impromptu traps using the environment and a successful Survival check or Craft if they have a specialization that would fit. Unless they take an action that gets them noticed by a drone before they strike, the Heroes can use the spread out nature of the machines to their advantage and try

Pursued by the Celedrones, the Heroes make their way through the woods towards Gemelos City.

to pick them off one by one. Once one of the drones is attacked, it alerts the rest and they move to the location as quickly as possible. The drones are programmed to use their taser dart attacks to subdue the Heroes, and while a successful hit to the head or chest could knock a hero out, the drones are treated as Rabble so they must rely on random Hit Location rolls. The drones use their Flight to their advantage, staying at least 3-5 meters in the air, so the Heroes need to use ranged attacks or look at other options to get to them. If more than half of their numbers are destroyed, the remaining drones attempt to break off and fly up to a higher altitude to regroup and await further orders from their owners. This gives the Heroes an opportunity to flee the area if they choose. With a single Core Power, no armor, and makeshift weapons there is a chance the Heroes

Core Power Unlocks Table

Power Level	Street	Epic	Paragon
Recommended number of encounters	1	2-3	3-5

Power Out..., er..., Onages?

The serum used on the Heroes breaks down as the Heroes experience stressful situations. Epic or Paragon level Heroes have significantly more Core Powers to unlock than Street level Heroes. The C.O.P. Alerts included below provide the Games Master with a means to prepare the Heroes with the power-ups they will need for the final battle. As a general rule of thumb, the Heroes' final Core Power should re-emerge immediately prior to the events in Revelations (page 24). Street level Heroes may require only one or two stressful encounters before reaching this point. Conversely, a Paragon level hero may need six encounters to unlock all but their final power slot. The Games Master should be mindful of the full number of Core Powers of each hero and adjust the number of encounters accordingly.

could be defeated by the drones if they engage them in combat. The taser darts used by the drones do little lasting damage and their effects are temporary, so the Heroes are able to recover and the Games Master should give them another chance to escape or a rematch against the drones.

• **They can hide**. The Heroes can attempt to stay hidden from the drones and wait for them to pass by. The drones use sensors that look for heat signatures and motion, so if the Heroes take measures to keep still or mask their heat, they might be able to avoid detection. This is treated as a Sorting Roll with the Heroes using Conceal (if they are masking themselves or another hero) or Stealth (if trying to remain still or keep cover between them and the sensor) against the drone's Perception. The Heroes have to roll against any drones that would pass by the area they are hiding in, or all against a single drone if they are in a small area. If the drone wins, it discovers one or more of the Heroes, and the others immediately converge on the location. If the Heroes win, they remain hidden until the drones pass by and exceed their search radius. Note that if the Heroes try to hide in or near the truck at least two drones remain once they reach it, making any Perception checks made to locate the Heroes one Difficulty Grade easier.

If the Heroes manage to destroy any of the drones and take time to examine the remains, they find no identifying symbols or markings linking them to any individual or organization. They can locate the drone's hard drive and a long-range transmitter that would also be a means to control the unit from a distance. With a successful Craft (Weapons) or Mechanisms roll, the Heroes can remove the taser dart launcher and use it as a weapon, and with a Craft (Armor) check a hero can take hull components and create some makeshift armor for 1d4 locations per drone with a Bulk of 0 and an Armor Rating of 2.

Whether they destroyed or evaded the drones, the Heroes remain in the middle of the woods with no idea where they are and how to get back to civilization. They can follow the dirt road back the way the truck came from, or they can travel through the forest. If they previously made a successful Navigation (forest) or Survival check, they would know if they travel West they move towards the coastline and have a better chance of locating a roadway or community. Whether by dirt road or forest, eventually the Heroes move up to a location with a higher elevation, and from there they can see the lights of an urban area in the distance. This is the suburb of the Crown district of Gemelos City, and after another two hours of walking the Heroes can reach it.

• *C.O.P. Alert – A River Runs Through It: During their travels through the woods the Heroes find their path blocked by a river swelled by recent rains and melting snow from higher elevations. While they could try to find a way around, it would significantly increase the time it would take for them to exit the forest and potentially lead to further encounters with the Celedrones. The river current is strong but not so strong that someone couldn't*

THE ROAD TO NOWHERE

The Heroes may decide to try to determine where the truck was headed, traveling the dirt road in the direction the vehicle was originally going. The facility the truck was headed to is over 50 km away, and the road branches off several times so it will be nearly impossible for Heroes to find their way there during the events of the adventure. Even Heroes with Core Powers such as Flight or Enhanced Speed have difficulty finding the location, and using abilities such as Postcognition or Technopathy on the drones does not give enough usable information to trace them back to their source. If the players persist in seeking it out, there are a few options to try to get them back on track with the adventure.

• Have the Heroes reach a spot where they see the outskirts of Gemelos City and suggest the truck was headed there.

• When the Heroes recover their memories, one of them experiences a flash that there is someone important to them that needs care and they need to get back to civilization as soon as possible.

• The Heroes locate a new landfill deep in the woods with a recently dug pit, and the numerous truck tracks leading there suggest they were going to be dumped at the location.

swim across, and this would be an Extended Task using Athletics. Heroes could also use Survival to create some makeshift ropes or a small raft from fallen logs. Depending on their Core Powers, the Heroes could also find creative ways to traverse the river: freezing it with Elemental Control, using Blast or Enhanced Strength to fell a tree, floating allies across with Telekinesis, and so forth.

• ***C.O.P. Alert – Roughing It**: While the Heroes are traveling through the woods, they can make a Perception check to notice someone in the distance crying out in panic. If they investigate, the Heroes stumble upon two Celedrones buzzing around a small campsite, firing taser darts into a tent. The cries are coming from Tobias and Daniel, a young couple who were out camping. The drones located them while searching for the Heroes and are following their programming to subdue any humanoid targets they discover. If the Heroes intervene and help the couple, they are grateful and offer to guide the Heroes back to civilization. Tobias and Daniel hiked up to their campsite, and with their help, the Heroes reach the edge of the city within an hour. Neither of them recognizes the Heroes and they don't have a lot of resources or information, and once they help the characters get back to civilization, the couple departs to head back to their apartment.*

WELCOME TO GEMELOS

When the Heroes reach the outskirts of Gemelos City it is still hours till dawn, but their long night is still not over. Read the following:

> *You stumble through the darkness for what seems like forever, but then suddenly you break through the forest and out into the edge of civilization. An actual paved road greets your weary eyes, and further down you can see streetlights surrounded by a small cloud of swirling bugs. Your fragmented memories don't register anything familiar, but at this point it is far better than being hunted by strange robots in the middle of the woods. The lights continue on, marking a pathway that will hopefully lead you to safety, shelter, and maybe some answers as to who you are and what happened to you.*

The Heroes have time to explore the edge of the Crown, which mainly consists of suburbs, shopping centers, and various local businesses. At this time of night the streets are mostly empty except for the rare night owl out on their own business. The Heroes have freedom to explore the suburbs if they would like, gather some information on their location, or scrounge for supplies such as clothing, masks (if the hero normally wore a mask, then they might have the wherewithal to realize they need one, even if they don't fully understand why), mundane gear, and weapons.

The section of the Crown where the Heroes emerge is nicknamed Prince Hills and it consists of industrial parks and upper middle-class neighborhoods. There are also businesses that serve the local community such as restaurants, shopping centers and malls, and various chain and independent shops. If the Games Master would like to provide some more detail to Prince Hills as the Heroes explore, they can use the Random Suburbs Events/Locations table found on page 34 to give the area some flavor or add places the Heroes can attempt to explore.

POWER OUTAGES

The medicine used to suppress the Heroes' Core Powers remains in their systems until they are fully able to flush it out. Even as they regain their special abilities, the Heroes find their powers don't always work as intended until they regain all their lost memories. To simulate this each hero has the Power Outage Limit (see *Destined* page 76) applied to all Core Powers that require a Skill check to activate or use. This Limit also applies to any special movement powers such as Enhanced Speed, Flight, or Teleport, or for any Core Power where the manifestation would not be part of the hero's normal state of being. For example, Torc's Inherent Armor power represents a mystical protection aura provided by his magical torc, so the Games Master determines it would be affected. Heroes with those types of Core Powers would need to make an Easy Willpower check as a Free Action, and if it is failed the power does not work. As per the rules for the Limit any failed check results in the Core Power not working for 1d6+1 minutes, but if the hero rolls a Fumble, they lose use of the power for 1d3+1 hours instead of days. This temporary Limit disappears as soon as the Heroes regain all their lost memories.

Since it's after midnight by the time they emerge from the woods, there are very few locations that are open to the public, and fewer still that would be accommodating to a band of unkempt people wearing muddy and torn unitards. If the Heroes enter a bar or an all-night chain retail store without cleaning up or getting proper clothes, they are likely to be turned away or have the police called on them. Contacting the police could also be problematic when the Heroes notice posters at bus stops and billboards displaying the slogan, *"Absolute Power Corrupts Absolutely. Report any unregistered X-Ns to the extranormal Response Unit at 310-555-5327,"* with the picture of a costumed vigilante behind bars. Thankfully the Heroes won't see many police patrols in Prince Hills at this time of night, but if they cause any problems or draw too much attention, they run the risk of the authorities coming to the scene. The Games Master may add to the tension by warning the Heroes about being too "out in the open."

The Heroes can keep a low profile, take their time searching the area, or hole up somewhere safe while trying to figure out their next move. This can also be a good time for them to get to know each other as best as they can with their lost memories, and get a handle on their powers. The Games Master is also welcome to add additional encounters to spice up the Heroes' down time. Each encounter should prove stressful enough to help trigger the re-emergence of another power (and Passion) for the Heroes. Here are a few suggestions:

• **C.O.P. Alert – Speed Racers**: *Two late night street racers are out cruising Prince Hills, looking for a good straight road. When they find one, it just so happens to be the street the Heroes are traveling down at that moment, so the Heroes hear and see the two souped up cars revving up before they start their race. The high speed on a two-lane main road is risky enough, but one of the cars begins losing control and clips the other vehicle. This sends them both off course, endangering both the cars and the Heroes. Avoiding a careening car is treated as a Intensity 3 Peril (see Destined, page 201) with a Potency rating of 60%, and Heroes need to Evade the car or find another creative solution, and if they Fail, they take 3d6 damage. If the cars are not stopped or redirected, the drivers will be severely injured and inflict serious property damage.*

• **C.O.P. Alert – Smartphonies**: *The Heroes notice some lights on in a cell phone store long after it should be closed. If they investigate they see a van marked Moonlight Cleaners parked on the side of the building and a man is loading boxes of new smartphones into the truck. Observing the scene more closely reveals several more people clearing out the store's merchandise, and a successful Perception check through the front windows notices another man holding a gun on the actual cleaning crew. A group of four crooks (use the Goon stats on page 321-22 of Destined) are robbing the store, and the Heroes can opt to foil the robbery. One robber is loading boxes from the back storeroom, two are clearing out the registers and taking floor models, and the last robber is watching over the two maintenance workers.*

• **C.O.P. Alert – Night Swimming**: *The Heroes pass by a local YMCA club and hear panicked screams coming from within. The club is locked but if they search around the building they find an unlocked window ajar on the side of the building. A group of local youths unlocked the window earlier that day, planning on coming back later for a night swim after hours. One of them struck his head on the diving board and was knocked out, and the rest of the group are trying to get him out of the pool, but he is too heavy for them to lift. If the Heroes investigate and discover what happened they only have a few moments to rescue the young man before he drowns.*

• **C.O.P. Alert – Heroes Helping Heroes**: *As the Heroes are making their way to their next destination they are passed by a number of emergency vehicles with sirens blaring. If the Heroes follow the responders, a few blocks away, a tenement building is engulfed in flame. A number of residents remain trapped within the building. This C.O.P. Alert can provide the Heroes with novel ways of utilizing their powers to rescue stranded victims safely. The Heroes should also remember that Gemelos City has an Extranormal Response Unit that may not look favorably on any Heroes caught "interfering" with rescue operations.*

• **C.O.P. Alert – Stick 'Em Up**: *As the Heroes explore Gemelos City, they make their way through Freedom Plaza, a prominent park in the Crown. As they walk down a dimly lit path they are accosted by 4 to 6 Goons (see Destined, pages 321-22) who demand that they hand over their wallets and valuables. Alternatively, they may come across a scene of a group of Goons demanding the same of a young couple. How do the Heroes respond to these muggers?*

• **C.O.P. Alert – Everybody on the Floor!**: *If the Heroes wait until the next day before venturing out into the city, they hear panicked screams coming from inside a bank as they walk past. The bank is being robbed by a group of eight masked Goons (see Destined, pages 321-22) armed with various firearms. Can the Heroes save the civilians inside?*

After some point when the Heroes are walking around outside, they notice the distinct hum of the Celedrones and see their scanning red lights in the distance. Even if they locate their tracking chips and find a way to remove them, the robots continue to search for them to find a way to recapture them. As the robots grow ever closer to their current location, read the following:

> *You see the drones all around you, growing closer each second. As you search for some way to get past them or somewhere to hide you are startled when a small, older-model hatchback comes to a screeching halt beside you. A young woman with curly hair leans out the driver's side window, speaking quickly as she says, "Thank God I found you! Get inside!"*

This is Callie Carter, a young conspiracy blogger who was working with one of the Heroes prior to their disappearance (see her stats on page 30). Which hero is up to the Games Master, and she addresses them directly. She is desperate to keep moving, eyeing the drones while she tries to get them inside her car. If they refuse or question her, she gets more desperate and answers questions quickly and tersely. If they do agree, she answers questions while they drive away, and she does her best to steer clear of any visible drones. A successful Insight check reveals she is not lying, and she reveals the following information to them:

• She works in IT support but she has also taken an interest in extranormals over the past few years. She believes they are good for the city and she has become an online activist who goes by the pseudonym "FREEP0WER." She attempts to build community support for X-Ns who help those in need, and to aid those same X-Ns with information and some white hat hacking.

• She became aware of the disappearances of X-Ns several months ago and has been attempting to uncover what was happening. She learned most of the disappearances were either not reported, or the Gemelos City Police Department ensured the reports were not released to the media. From her best estimate at least 30 people who possessed powers have disappeared.

• She learned about the robots' part in the disappearances after locating a witness's smartphone video on an internet forum. It shows

Having obtained some less conspicuous clothes, the Heroes make their way stealthily through the backstreets of the city.

one of the Celedrones chasing someone across the rooftops of the Ossuary. While she has not been able to trace the source of the robots, she did find a reference to someone or something called "Praxagore" on an anti-extranormals message board, but she hasn't yet been able to track that down aside from the reference to the ancient Greek physician Praxagoras

• The hero she knows contacted her after discovering they were both seeking out the missing people. The hero was acting as her field agent in tracking down leads. She lost contact with the hero a week ago when they were following-up on a sighting of one of the drones in Prince Hills and she has been searching the area each night hoping to find some trace of her ally.

• She engineered a makeshift signal detector in the hopes she would locate one of the drones during her search and use it to trace them back to their source. As yet she hasn't been successful, and

> ### "WE PREFER TO WALK"
>
> It's entirely possible the Heroes may refuse to go with Callie no matter how much she pleads, either because they don't trust her or because of concerns for her safety. If the Heroes are adamant in refusing her help, she won't stick around but she tosses them a burner smartphone with a contact number for her burner phone. She tells them to call if they need help or information before she speeds off. This alters some aspects of the remaining encounters so here are some suggestions to keep the adventure on track:
>
> • The Heroes can stumble upon the robbery at the convenience store in the next encounter while they are traveling around. The encounter plays out as normal after that without Callie being involved.
>
> • Dr. Julian happens to shop at the same store when the encounter occurs. If the Heroes display their powers or are injured, he approaches them and offer his services as a doctor. This leads into the events that start on page 19.

any signals used by the robots are lost in the morass of transmissions over a busy urban area. If the Heroes have not located their tracking implants, Callie's signal detector picks them up as soon as they get in her car and she can use the device to pinpoint their location. If the Heroes defeated any of the drones and took components from them, Callie can use the parts to isolate the signals of the Celedrones after an hour of work.

Callie is able to help the Heroes with information about Gemelos City and the current status of the communities there, and her expertise with Electronics and Computers can also help them gain information on any devices they took from the truck or any of the robots. Unfortunately she doesn't know much about the hero she was working with because of their short association, but what she does know is enough to allow that hero to make a Willpower check. If successful, it triggers more of that hero's lost memories and they regain a second Passion and some memories about their career as a hero (fighting street criminals, memories of their costume, and so on). The Passion gained should be one that is related to the hero's motivations for fighting crime.

INCONVENIENT CONVENIENCE

The time spent searching for the Heroes used up most of Callie's fuel for her car, and not long after they all set off together read the following:

> *Callie is driving like a woman possessed, and you see her eyes darting back and forth from the road to her rear-view mirror. You can still see the distant red cones of light from the drones searching for you, thankfully growing more distant with each passing second. Then Callie shouts, "Dammit!" and you see her glaring at the dashboard. "We need to stop and get some gas or we aren't getting out of here," she says, punctuating the sentence with an angry jab at the low fuel warning light that just appeared. Up ahead you see the lights of a 24 hour store called Coastal Convenience and with a jerk of the wheel she steers the car into the parking lot and up to the gas pumps.*

Callie gets out to pump gas and she asks the Heroes to get some food or drinks before they get back on the road, handing them some cash. Callie doesn't really have a specific destination or plan aside from getting them all as far from the drones as possible, so she asks that they hurry so they can get going. When the Heroes enter the store, read the following:

> *The automatic doors slide open and you hear a small chime somewhere in the store. The bright fluorescent lights seem blinding after the night you've been having, but your stomach grumbles when you see the brightly colored packaging of junk food and your nose picks up the smell of day-old hot dogs spinning on heated rollers. Not the best fare, but at this point anything sounds good. An older man in a store uniform with a name tag reading "Roger" stands behind the counter and he gives you a quick nod and forced smile as you walk in.*

Have any of the Heroes inside the store make an Insight check. If successful, they notice something off about Roger's body language, specifically how he is trying to hide how tense and nervous he is. Just before they arrived, a young man entered the store with a pistol and was in the process of robbing it, but when Callie's car pulled up he jumped behind the counter and is currently crouched down next to Roger. There is also a woman named Sylvia who was using the restroom, but when she heard the robber threaten Roger she went back in the bathroom to hide and called the police.

The robber is a scared and desperate young man named Quentin who is in debt to the Vallo Crime Family for some gambling debts. Feeling like he had no other option, he figured he could get some quick cash by robbing the store and pay off the enforcer he owes, but now he is panicking. Astute Heroes can make a Perception check and if successful they see Quentin hiding next to the clerk on one of the security monitors behind the counter. How they react to the situation determines how the robber acts. Here are a few viable options:

- **Aggression**: The Heroes may go on the attack, either verbally or physically. They may try to gain surprise by tricking the robber into thinking they are not aware of his presence, intimidate him into giving up, or leap over the counter and try to stop him before he hurts someone. If combat ensues, Quentin uses the statistics of a Goon from the core rulebook. While he is not an inherently violent man, Quentin panics and lashes out, especially if the Heroes display their powers. The risk of this approach is Roger could easily get caught in the crossfire of any violent action, or Quentin might try to take him hostage if the Heroes present themselves as aggressive.

- **Diplomacy**: The Heroes may try to talk the robber out of his plan. If the Heroes make Quentin aware they know he is there, he pops up and holds Roger at gunpoint. However, Quentin is not inherently a violent man. He can be talked down with successful Deception and Influence checks as part of an Extended Task against Quentin's Insight and Willpower of 40%. If the Heroes learn why he is trying to rob the store and seem sympathetic to his plight, the Heroes make these checks at one Difficulty Grade easier. If he is successfully talked down, Quentin tries to flee the scene without incident if the Heroes let him or reluctantly submit to being bound for the police if he feels he has no better option.

The Heroes' friend Callie has been searching the city for them since their disappearance some days ago.

- **Ignorance**: The Heroes may simply choose to ignore the situation, either because they don't want to get involved or they feel their own issues take priority over a robbery. If they act like nothing's wrong and leave the store, Quentin lays low until he thinks they are gone and finishes taking what he can carry from the register when he thinks the coast is clear. While it is not the most heroic approach, it may be the one that makes the most sense to them at that time.

- **Powers**: Depending on what Core Powers the Heroes have, they may be able to intervene using them to their advantage. Empathy or Telepathy could get inside the robber's head, a display of Blast or Enhanced Strength could scare Quentin into giving up, or using Creation or Force Field between him and the clerk could keep innocent

Quentin the robber intends to hold up the Coastal Convenience store as his only option to save his neck from the vengeance of Vallo Crime Family goons The appearance of the Heroes puts a crimp in his plans.

lives safe. The Games Master should give the Heroes the opportunity to use their Core Powers to feel like true Heroes in the situation.

No matter how the Heroes resolve the situation, when the woman in the restroom called the police it was intercepted by receivers in the Celedrones around the area and redirected to their owners. They have been monitoring calls in the area and have remained on the line with her, pretending to be an emergency services call center. Sylvia gives descriptions of the Heroes and talks about any displays of powers she sees, and this causes the owners to dispatch some Celedrones and a TALOS (Tactical Automated Logistics/Operations Servitor) combat robot (see page 28) to the site immediately to intercept and recapture the Heroes. Read the following:

> You walk back into the crisp night air and see Callie is just finishing up refueling her car. She waves you over before something in the sky draws her attention away. You look up to see a small swarm of red lights descending on the store, all surrounding a larger object that is emitting white-hot exhaust from its back. With a sudden crash that shakes the pavement under your feet a massive metallic robot lands between you and Callie, its single eye glowing a fierce red. The small swarm flies around it, more of the same drones that you encountered in the forest. In a cold monotone voice the large robot says, "Surrender immediately and submit to re-processing. You have five seconds to comply." With that a digital countdown appears on its optic processor, quickly ticking down as you hear something on the robot begin to charge up.

One Celedrone flies in for each hero, and they primarily serve as air support for the larger robot. The TALOS Unit abides by its countdown and if the Heroes do surrender, whether as a ruse or to prevent any innocents from being endangered, it commands the Celedrones fly in to attempt to bind the Heroes' wrists using their grasper claws. Tricking the robots requires an opposed Deception roll against the large robot's Insight, and if successful the Heroes can gain a surprise attack against the machines. If the roll is unsuccessful, or if the Heroes refuse to surrender, try to escape, or take aggressive action, combat begins. The robots use the following strategies during the combat:

• The TALOS Unit uses its stun blaster at range as long as it can, attempting to disable the Heroes quickly and efficiently. If engaged in melee combat, it uses its powerful fists to try to batter any Heroes close to it into submission.

• The Celedrones fly around the parking lot, trying to keep out of range of melee attacks while firing their taser darts at any hero in range.

• If the TALOS Unit suffers a Serious Wound in any location and any Celedrones are left, one of the drones flies to that Hit Location on its next turn and its chassis reconfigures so it can merge with the large robot. This adds 3 Hit Points to the damaged location and increases its Armor Rating by 1 for the remainder of the encounter.

• If all the Celedrones are destroyed, or if the TALOS Unit is in danger of being Incapacitated, the remaining robots attempt to flee the scene by flying away on their next turn. If the TALOS Unit is Incapacitated, it activates a self-destruct sequence on its next turn: after 1d3 Combat Rounds a white-hot localized blast inflicts 3d6 damage to 1d4+1 Hit Locations on anyone unfortunate enough to be within 2 meters of the robot.

Callie does not directly get involved in the combat, but if the Heroes are in trouble, she attempts to ram the TALOS robot with her car to disable it. Anyone left inside the store remains there, watching the battle and taking footage of it on their smartphones. If the Heroes saved Roger from the robber, he also tries to help if they are in trouble by trying to distract the robots by shouting at them. The robots will not target Callie or any other innocent bystander unless directly attacked, and then they resort to non-lethal means to disable them.

The Heroes also need to be careful around the fuel pumps during the battle. A Fumble with a Core Power or attack that could potentially ignite gasoline could be devastating, although Heroes not concerned with property damage could also use this as a strategy against the robots if desperate. The parking lot also has cover and places to hide in the form of concrete barriers, sturdy waste bins, and up to three other cars (if Quentin didn't escape). If the Heroes can defeat or drive off the robots, and if Callie is not injured or her car is wrecked, she tells them they should get back on the road immediately, as they can all now hear police sirens approaching. After witnessing their second Core Powers emerge, and if the Heroes tell her about the problems they are having (See Power Outages on page 13), she has an idea of someone who might be able to figure out what is going on with the Heroes.

The Doctor Is In

Callie has made many contacts during her crusade to help extranormals, and one of them is a physician and researcher named Dr. Carl Julian.

> ### Second Power and Passion
>
> The arrival of the robots causes enough stress to trigger the emergence of a second Core Power and another Passion. Alternatively, if the Games Master has the Heroes engage in C.O.P. Alerts, they can allow the Heroes to regain their second Core Powers before this encounter, but the second Passion still unlocks at this time. Just like before, the hero gains a power of their choice along with any Boosts and Limits depending on the creation method. For Heroes with four or more Core Powers, they now regain two of their lost abilities. They also regain the second highest value Passion, and it triggers memories that would be associated with it, though as before the hero can also choose to roll on an appropriate Background table as well. If a hero already regained a second Passion from meeting Callie, they only regain a Core Power at this time.

She met him in an online forum. There they began talking about the science behind the Godstrand and stayed connected after he told her he had great interest in helping those with powers. He also told her to refer anyone who was having concerns or difficulties with their powers to him and he would do his best to guide them through it. If the Heroes are willing, she calls Dr. Julian and he asks her to bring the Heroes to his clinic in the Woodchurch neighborhood immediately. When they arrive, read the following:

> *You make your way several miles across town until you arrive at the address Dr. Julian provided. The clinic is an older three-story building set far off the main road, surrounded by a small stone wall. It has the look of an old hospital or institution, but the newer windows and updated HVAC systems on the roof show off the renovations made to keep it up to date. You pass by a large sign that reads "JDJ Biotech" and you see a middle aged man with thinning hair and glasses waiting for you at the main entrance.*

Callie and the Heroes arrive at the headquarters of JDJ Biotech, where geneticist and biochemist Dr Carl Julian may be able to help the Heroes find answers as to what has happened to them.

This is Dr. Carl Julian (see his stats on page 29), an expert in genetics and biochemistry. Unbeknownst to them, he is also the one who is responsible for the Heroes losing their powers. His daughter Julia was affected by the initial wave of the Awakening, but she was unable to control her destructive powers and a blast of energy caused the roof of her apartment building to collapse, killing her instantly. Dr. Julian never got over her death and while he maintained the facade of being a respectable scientist with an academic interest in studying the Godstrand phenomenon, in truth he was seeking a way to eradicate whatever it was that caused people to develop powers.

He was approached by a mysterious benefactor six months prior who offered him an unfinished sample of a serum that could suppress Core Powers in extranormals. They also gave him access to advanced equipment in his lab and robot servitors that help him get unwilling test subjects to help perfect the serum. Dr. Julian's end goal was a formula that would completely eliminate the Godstrand and the powers it manifests, and if it happened to kill those afflicted with it, that was acceptable to him. The Heroes were the latest victims of his twisted experiments, plucked off the streets of Gemelos City by the robots, and they were being shipped off by his benefactors to a location unknown to him when their transport malfunctioned. Dr. Julian frequented social media sites used by extranormals and sympathizers to their cause to help locate potential subjects, and he saw Callie as a perfect unwitting pawn to lead him to more victims.

Callie explains how the Heroes' powers are malfunctioning when she contacts him, and Dr. Julian's plan is to present himself as a potential Ally to the Heroes to lull them into a false sense of security. Under the guise of a friendly scientist, he tries to get them to agree to some blood tests and brain scans to get the data he needs on why his latest batch of serum isn't working. Once he has the data he needs, he plans to invite the Heroes to wait in a specially prepared meeting room outfitted with systems that pump anesthetic gas through the air vents to knock them out. Once Incapacitated, he will have his Celedrones take them to the building's incinerator to dispose of any evidence before going back to the drawing board with the serum's development.

While that is his plan, it is most likely not a scenario the Heroes will be happy with. How things transpire depends on how trusting the Heroes are of him and if they see through his facade. While they might initially trust Callie's recommendation and give him the benefit of the doubt, there are a few points where the Heroes can see the cracks in his persona.

• If the Heroes take time to ask him about his educational background and credentials, he openly discusses his education at Aletheia University, his work at Pandora Pharmaceuticals, and how he was a colleague of Dr. Echidna, the scientist who first posited the idea of the Godstrand. If they get him talking about his research into the Godstrand, or ask him about his family or what the name of the company means (it is named after his deceased daughter Julia Darlene Julian), he must make a Deception check against the Insight of whoever is asking. If he succeeds, he talks about the Godstrand and his late daughter without any anger coming through, but if the hero succeeds they pick up on some underlying animosity he has towards the Godstrand, as well as extranormals.

• If the Heroes tell Dr. Julian about waking in the tubes and the crashed truck, he asks them questions to get more information about why the truck crashed and where they were when it happened. His interest in the details behind the crash might give them pause if they make successful Insight checks.

• While in his lab or if the Heroes consent to testing, Dr. Julian takes notes and enter data he collects on a laptop he keeps on a rolling cart. Observant Heroes can make a Perception check, and if successful they notice the data he is entering on them seems to be part of a pre-existing file, even though he claims this is the first time he has met them.

When he hears of the events of the night, Dr Julian is deeply concerned.

SUSPECTED

If the Heroes observe some things that make them suspicious of Dr. Julian and confront him about the discrepancies, he does his best (and use his Deception Skill) to try to come up with excuses for his responses or another reason for something they witnessed. He might claim his anger is a result of his grief about his daughter, say his interest in the circumstances of the crash was out of curiosity, and the files on his laptop are not specifically related to the Heroes but are part of a larger database he keeps on Godstrand research. If the Heroes are dissuaded or don't take immediate action, he still proceeds with the testing if they permit and the encounter continues as detailed below. If the Heroes remain suspicious and refuse to allow him to proceed, his facade drops as his frustration mounts. Read the following:

The Heroes make their escape from the anesthetic gas in Dr Julian's trapped conference room.

> **The kindness in Dr. Julian's face falls away like a mask, replaced by a scowl. "You and your damned kind just can't make things easy, can you? Don't you realize I am trying to help you? I'm trying to cure you of this plague that afflicts you, freeing you from these abilities you have been cursed with! If you're going to be difficult, then I'll just need to get what I can from your cadavers." All around you, cabinets fly open and seemingly mundane pieces of equipment shift with mechanical whirring, revealing more of the drones that have been plaguing you since you first woke up from your unwanted slumber. The robots form a barrier between you and the doctor, protecting him as he runs back towards a door marked as the stairwell.**

Dr. Julian releases two battle Celedrones for each hero, and the robots move to intercept anyone who attempts to attack him or capture him before he reaches the door. The Games Master can also spend one of Dr. Julian's Luck Points to cause some other contrivance to prevent the Heroes from stopping his escape to the roof (a drone bursting out of a cabinet knocks it over, blocking the hero, and so forth). The robots attack in a straightforward manner, trying to disable the Heroes if possible by targeting limbs. The lab has many machines and long tables that can serve as cover, and clever Heroes can use the medical equipment there to cause distractions or help disable the drones. There are volatile chemicals, powerful magnets in the brain scanners, and high voltage electrical lines that can all be used if needed to create Perils (see *Destined*, page 201). If the Heroes manage to defeat the drones, move on to the next section.

COMPLIANCE

If the Heroes do not discern anything fishy about Dr. Julian and are compliant with his requests, he draws blood and run a short brain scan on each of them. Once they are all finished, he invites the Heroes and Callie to sit in a small conference room to wait for him to analyze the blood samples he collected. After entering the room, he offers to get them some tea and coffee while they wait and he closes the door. Have the Heroes roll Perception checks, and anyone who is successful hears the faint clicking noise of the door locking and the ventilation system kicks on in the room. Dr. Julian previously rigged the room up to a bypass system that allows him to pump in various gases to pacify unruly subjects, and he fills the room with an anesthetic that renders the Heroes unconscious in a few moments. Read the following:

> *There is a slight crackle as a loudspeaker in the room turns on. You hear Dr. Julian's voice fill the room. "I am truly sorry for this, but it and my deception are necessary. Ever since my dear daughter Julia's life was cut short by this damned curse they call the Godstrand, I have been trying to find a way to cure all of you of your affliction. I apologize for making you unwilling subjects for my serum, and I am sorry it didn't work. Be thankful you have given me valuable data to help the next iteration of my formula. Pray that I find better luck with the next group of subjects, and know your sacrifice will not be in vain."*

The gas has a slight medicinal smell that quickly becomes apparent as precious seconds tick away. The Heroes need to find a way to stop the gas or escape the room before they are overcome. They can take 1d3+1 Actions before the gas starts to affect them, and after that time has passed they must make Endurance checks. The first check is at Easy Difficulty, and each successive check becomes one Difficulty Grade harder. Anyone who fails is rendered unconscious for 1d3+1 hours unless revived with a successful First Aid or Medicine check in an area with normal air. Any hero with a Core Power that removes their need to breathe (Life Support or Artificial Being) is immune to the gas, and any that acquired a piece of equipment such as a gas mask are also safe. The Heroes have a few options to get free from the room:

- **Break open the door**: The Heroes can try to smash open the door. The door has 4 Armor Points and the Heroes need to inflict 10 Hit Points of damage to break the lock and get it open.

- **Disable the lock**: Heroes with the Mechanisms Skill can attempt to disable or pick the lock to get the door open. Without the proper tools this is a

> ## REMAINING CORE POWERS AND PASSION
>
> If the Heroes are trapped in the locked room or if Dr. Julian sics his drones on them, they have endured enough stress to flush the remainder of the power dampening serum from their bodies. At this time the Heroes regain any remaining Core Powers, including Boosts and Limits, and the last of their Passions. They also regain all their lost memories, including their real names, history, and any allies, contacts, rivals, and enemies from their lives. If the players are willing, they can leave some details of their former lives blank (a side effect of the serum) and build them as part of the ongoing storyline after this adventure is complete.

Hard check, but Callie keeps a multi-tool in her bag which makes the check Normal.

- **Break the window**: The one-way glass is reinforced but it can still be shattered. It has 3 Armor Points and inflicting at least 6 Hit Points of damage shatters it enough for someone to get through.

- **Stop the flow of gas**: The Heroes can try to use items of clothing or furniture to block the air vent. Unless it is a perfect seal, this only slows the gas flow down, but it buys the Heroes 1d3+1 more Actions before they need to make Endurance checks.

- **Powers**: Heroes can use their fantastic Core Powers, and if they do not, Callie tries to encourage them to use whatever abilities they have to get free. How they accomplish this depends on what powers they have, but the Games Master should allow them to be creative.

If the Heroes are unable to get free and succumb to the gas, the Games Master should give them another chance. Perhaps the gas is not as effective as it should be and they only remain unconscious for a few minutes, waking up as several Celedrones attempt to move them to the incinerator downstairs in the building for disposal. If the Heroes are able to get free from the room, they witness Dr. Julian head out the door to the stairwell and blocking their path are one battle Celedrone for each hero. If they are able to defeat them, move on to the next section.

Power Outage

REVELATIONS

If the Heroes follow Dr. Julian to the stairwell, read the following:

> *The door Dr. Julian fled through opens up to an ascending staircase and you hear sounds from a door above you just before it slams shut with a heavy thud. When you arrive and open it, you find yourselves on the building's rooftop. The wind is whipping around, stirred up by the arrival of more of the damned drones you have been dealing with and another one of the larger, humanoid robots. The larger machine's chest is split open, and you see Dr. Julian inside, wearing the robot like a massive suit of armor. As its chest hatch closes you hear his voice, distorted by the robot's sound systems. "You and your kind are just another damned plague, a disease afflicting this world! You took my daughter, and I was so close to finding a way to rid the world of your unholy presence once and for all! No one should have to suffer like I did, and tonight I'll make sure no one ever suffers again!" Again you hear the robot's systems power up, but something tells you this time its weaponry will not be non-lethal.*

Dr. Julian fully embraces his villainous nature as Praxagore and is infuriated by their survival, but he is also frightened that if they are not killed it will expose his research and crimes. He has a modified TALOS Unit that allows him to operate it from within like a suit of powered battle armor. Using the abilities of the robot (see page 28), he attempts to destroy the Heroes, supported by four battle Celedrones.

If the Heroes don't follow, Dr. Julian still uses the armor feature of the TALOS Unit and waits for them to leave the building before flying down to confront the Heroes, delivering the same speech as above before attacking. Praxagore uses the following tactics during battle:

• He uses the robot's ranged attacks to keep his distance from the Heroes, picking them off one by one or blasting the rooftop to try to drop them down into the building. The roof has 6 Armor Points and if he can cause 10 Hit Points of damage it opens a hole big enough to drop someone through. The hero can make an Evade or Acrobatics check as an Action to avoid this. Failure results in a fall 5 meters to the level below.

• If the Heroes close with him, he attempts to smash them with the robot's strength, but he is not skilled with Unarmed, so he removes himself from close combat if he can. If the Heroes cause a Serious Wound to his weapons array, he resorts to Unarmed attacks out of desperation.

• Praxagore is also not skilled with flying the robot, but if things are looking desperate for him he takes to the air and use ranged attacks from there. The thrusters for its flight systems are located in the legs, and if either leg takes enough damage to suffer a Serious Wound, make an Athletics check. If he succeeds, he maintains control, but if he fails, the flight system malfunctions and he rockets off into the distance, completely out of control. His fate is left to the Games Master if this happens.

• The Celedrones offer air support when needed, but their primary role will be to repair any damage to the robot by merging with it as detailed above (page 18).

If Callie is on the roof with the Heroes, she takes cover and tries to keep out of the way. If Praxagore believes the Heroes have an attachment to her, he may try to endanger her or take her hostage if he needs to escape. While Callie is not a combatant, she is very skilled with Computers and Electronics, so if the Heroes are having difficulty, she can use her Skills to support their attack rolls against the robots and Praxagore by offering suggestions on weak points in their systems such as joints, optic systems, or the rotor.

If the Heroes are able to defeat Praxagore and he doesn't rocket off as detailed above, they can attempt to interrogate him to discover the details of his plot using the rules as presented on pages 192-194 of *Destined*. His animosity towards them and extranormals in general is palpable, and he is quite open about his desire to eradicate all traces of them from the world even if they do not successfully interrogate him. If they are successful, he talks about all the previous powered individuals he kidnapped and experimented on, and how he was given the base version of his serum from an unknown patron who also provided him with his robot minions (see Praxagore's Patron).

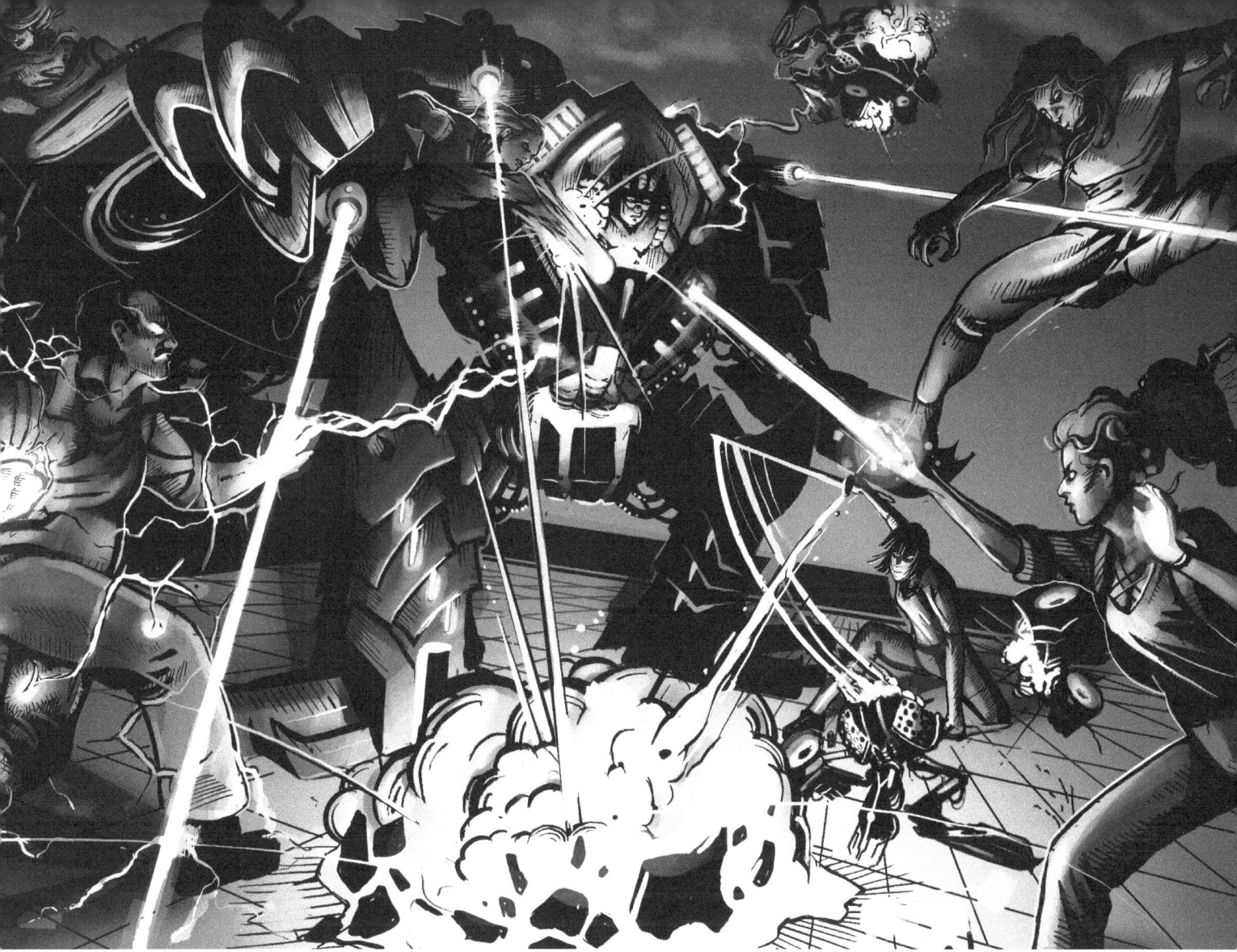

The Heroes, now restored to their full powers, confront Dr Julian on the roof of the JDJ building.

If Callie is present, she uses her smartphone to record what Dr. Julian says as evidence, and if the Heroes take time to explore Praxagore's lab, they can uncover the following information on his laptop with a successful Computers check:

• Dr. Julian tracked his progress with the serum over several different variations (the current version used on the Heroes is dubbed "Batch 14") and he gives a detailed chemical formula for each batch. The early versions only caused discomfort in subjects, the 11th batch caused violent and lethal allergic reactions to those with the Godstrand (to which he added the notation "very promising alternative"), and the last version dampened Core Powers but did not eliminate them. The information contained about his different serums could be valuable to the right people, but it could also be very dangerous in the wrong hands.

• He also kept files on each test subject, never noting their names but assigning each a letter and a number (the Heroes were the letter N with numbers going up to the total number of players). If the Heroes count up the totals, he kidnapped 47 test subjects before them. If asked during a successful interrogation, he reveals 13 of those subjects died and were disposed of in his building's incinerator and the remainder were taken away by his unknown patron to an unknown location via the same automated trucks the Heroes woke up in.

• Dr. Julian also kept personal logs on his computer, most of them rants about extranormals or grief-stricken missives about his deceased daughter and his nihilistic view on the world. There are also discussions about wanting to know more about his patron, talking about his dream of a world without powered individuals, and his

Power Outage

> ## Praxagore's Patron
>
> Dr. Julian is a medical doctor and research biochemist, not a robotics expert. He lacks the resources to fund and create the technology he used the experiment with his serum, and if the Heroes interrogate him he reveals he was approached anonymously by a sympathetic patron who took interest in his research. He was provided with the robots used to capture X-Ns, an early version of his serum, and advanced research equipment, but he never met directly with anyone from whoever was funding his operation. They would contact him via telephone, the number always listed as "unknown." Praxagore is the main villain of the adventure, but the identity of whoever was behind his scheme is intentionally left open-ended so the Games Master can expand upon this adventure if the Heroes wish to discover who is targeting the X-Ns of Gemelos City. Some possible culprits from the setting are:
>
> Kadre, a criminal group of information brokers. When they learned of Dr. Julian's experiments (and his hatred of X-Ns), they saw the potential and profits of having access to a formula that would strip people of their special powers. They offered to fund his research and provided special drones and battle robots they use in the field when necessary.
>
> Dr. Vellaro, the robotics expert and archenemy of the Fearless Force, has been seeking a way to strip his hated nemeses of their powers so he can finally defeat them once and for all. He took interest in Dr. Julian and provided some newer model combat robots so he could aid the doctor's research while also field testing his latest creations.
>
> Baron Malycer has always been jealous of those with inherent superpowers, so he decided to invest in Dr. Julian to see if he could take away the special abilities of others to make himself the superior being. He developed the technology based on designs he stole from a start-up robotics defense contractor he bought out.
>
> The Games Master can use any of the above or use a villain or villainous organization of their own creation, making this adventure the start of a long-ranging plot in a war on extranormals.

training using the battle armor model of the TALOS robots so he could "*feel an X-N's last breath as I use the robot's hands to crush the life out of them.*"

The lab is set far away enough from the local community that sounds and sights of the Heroes' battle against Praxagore would not be witnessed by anyone, so it would not be likely that the police would have been called. If Praxagore is alive and with the Heroes, they need to decide what to do with him. At this point the Heroes have all their memories, and a successful Easy Streetwise check reveals that the Gemelos City police do not take kindly to vigilante activity from extranormals and the Heroes might be arrested alongside the villain. Praxagore could be left Incapacitated at the lab, alongside any evidence collected and he will be taken in for his many crimes. If the Heroes are unsure about contacting the authorities, Callie offers to call and she keeps their names and identities out of things as best she can. She also remains an Ally for each hero if they choose to stay connected with her, offering services as a white hat hacker and as a source of information on the extranormal community in the city. With the villain defeated, the Heroes are now free to explore who they were and who they will be moving forward in Gemelos City.

Antagonists and Allies

Celedrones

Celedrones are tactical robots designed for observation and combat. They are about the size of a large dog and have a large central rotor for lift and several smaller rotors for thrust and fine maneuvering. Celedrones have a single sensor array on the front capable of video and audio recording and powerful infrared systems coupled with an infrared light that can be projected below the machine. They are built to be modular so different equipment and weapon systems can be attached to their chassis, although they are not terribly durable and lightly armored. Celedrones are designed to work with the heavier TALOS combat robot, serving as field support, but their bodies can also alter their shape to clamp onto the TALOS Unit to strengthen damaged locations, enhance its armor, or provide it with different weapon options as detailed below.

Celedrones

Action Points:	2
Damage Modifier:	None
Power Points:	-
Movement:	10 meters Flight
Initiative Bonus:	+8
Armor:	Polymer casing

Skills: Athletics 45%, Brawn 35%, Endurance 50%, Evade 45%, Perception 50%, Unarmed 45%

Abilities: *Artificial Being:* Celedrones are immune to any effect that would target a biological being or a sentient mind.
Flight: Celedrones can fly at a speed of 10 meters per move in combat, or 50 km/hr. outside of combat.
Heightened Senses: Celedrones can see in the infrared spectrum.

Hit Locations

1d20	Location	AP/HP
1-3	Right Rear Rotor	2/3
4-6	Left Rear Rotor	2/3
7-9	Main Body	4/5
10-12	Weapon Mount	3/3
13-15	Right Front Rotor	2/3
16-18	Left Front Rotor	2/3
19-20	Sensor Array	1/3

Combat Style

Evil Robot: 50%

Pacification Attacks

Attack	Size/Force	Range	Damage	AP/HP
Gripper Claw	S	-	1d4	6/8
Taser Dart Launcher	S	10/25/50	1d3	-

Incapacitating: if the taser dart inflicts damage the target is unable to take Actions or Reactions as long as the dart remains in them. See page 132 of *Destined* for more information.

Battle Attacks

Attack	Size/Force	Range	Damage	AP/HP
Gripper Claw	S	-	1d4	6/8
Pulse Laser	L	10/30/120	1d8+1	-

Notes:

Street Level Celedrones: If you are using Street Level Heroes, treat the Celedrones as Rabble. They are disabled after suffering 3 Hit Points of damage to any location, and their Skill values can't be higher than 40%.

Paragon Level Celedrones: If you are using Paragon Level Heroes, add an additional 1d3+1 Celedrones to any encounter that features them.

TALOS (Tactical Automated Logistics/Operations Servitor) Unit

TALOS units are humanoid robots designed for battlefield support. They stand 3 meters tall and have large, bulky bodies that also house the robot's sensors in a rotating cone on top, giving them an almost egg-shaped appearance. Their limbs are short and thick, with arms ending in powerful but flexible digits, and they are capable of lifting up to a small car with ease. TALOS units have weapon mounts on their shoulders and backs that are designed to be modular so the unit's loadout can be changed easily depending on the tactical situation. While they appear extremely durable, the robots only have moderate armor to allow them to remain maneuverable. They have limited AI but extensive combat software, allowing them to adapt to changing conditions on a battlefield. Some TALOS units also have a special modification that allows them to hold a single person inside their chassis, allowing this individual to use the robot like a powerful exoskeleton.

TALOS Drones

Action Points: 3
Damage Modifier: +1d6
Power Points: 12
Movement: 6 meters, 10 meters Flight
Initiative Bonus: +12
Armor: Polymer casing

Skills: Athletics 65%, Brawn 60%, Endurance 70%, Evade 45%, Perception 60%, Unarmed 65%

Abilities: Artificial Being: TALOS Units are immune to any effect that would target a biological being or a sentient mind.
Enhanced Strength: TALOS Units have a base lift of 1000 kg.
Flight: TALOS Units can fly at a speed of 10 meters per move in combat, or 50 km/hr. outside of combat.
Heightened Senses: TALOS Units can see in the infrared spectrum.

Hit Locations

1d20	Location	AP/HP
1-3	Right Leg	3/6
4-6	Left Leg	3/6
7-9	Torso	5/7
10-12	Weapon Mount	4/8
13-15	Right Arm	3/5
16-18	Left Arm	3/5
19-20	Sensors	3/6

Combat Style

Evil Robot: 65%

Pacification Attacks

Attack	Size/Force	Range	Damage	AP/HP
Robot Punch	L	-	1d4+1d6	-
Stun Blast	L	10/30/120	1d4+1d6	-

Stunning Blast: A location hit is subjected to the Stun Location Special Effect (see page 162 of the core rulebook)

Celedrone Repair and Modular Weaponry: The TALOS Unit is designed to work in concert with

Battle Attacks

Attack	Size/Force	Range	Damage	AP/HP
Robot Punch	L	-	1d4+1d6	6/20
Pulse Laser	H	30/100/300	2d6+2	-
Micro-Rockets	H	10/30/120	2d6+4	-

The robot can fire one barrage of Micro-Rockets that target a radius of 3 meters around the point of impact.

Celedrones, and as an Action a Celedrone can merge with the TALOS Unit to do the following:

• *Repair*: If the Celedrone attaches to a damaged Hit Location it repairs up to 3 Hit Points of damage.

• *Rotor Arm*: If the Celedrone attaches to an arm, its central rotor becomes a buzzsaw-like weapon, increasing the base Unarmed damage from 1d4 to 1d6+1.

• *Weapon Systems*: If the Celedrone attaches to the Weapon Mount Hit Location it adds its weapon system to those currently available to the TALOS Unit, granting it an extra Action Point that can only be used to fire the Celedrone's ranged weapon.

Notes:

Street Level TALOS Unit: If you are using Street level Heroes, lower the TALOS Unit's Skills to 50%, reduce its Damage Modifier to 1d4, and reduce its Armor by 1 in all Hit Locations.

Paragon Level TALOS Unit: If you are using Paragon level Heroes, increase the TALOS Unit's Action Points to 4, raise its Skills by 10%, increase its Damage Modifier to 1d8, and increase its Armor by 1 and Hit Points by 3 in all Hit Locations. The Battle units also gain an additional use of its micro-missile attack.

Dr. Carl Julian/Praxagore

Considered one of the greatest minds in biomedical research and the development of new pharmaceuticals, Dr. Carl Julian is also a person with deep rooted anger related to a tragic event in his past. After his wife's death of natural causes, his entire life revolved around his beloved daughter Julia, and she was just getting ready to start college when the Awakening occurred. Julia was one of the select people at the time who manifested abilities from the latent Godstrand DNA present in her body, and her powers involved the release of powerful waves of raw concussive force. Unfortunately, she had no control over this ability when it first manifested, and a burst of energy erupted out and collapsed the roof of her new apartment, killing her instantly and injuring several other people. Dr. Julian never got over her death, focusing a lot of his research on learning about the Godstrand and the people affected by it. His goal was not so much to understand how it worked, but to find a way to destroy it at all costs so no one had to suffer like he did. He insinuated himself in various online communities for extranormal sympathizers to get more information, and this is how both Callie Carter and his unknown patron located him. His patron promised him resources to help him in his quest, and they also provided an early version of a serum that was being developed to suppress powers in people with the Godstrand. Desperate to perfect it and fulfill his goals, Dr. Julian began kidnapping extranormals he located through online communities to test his formulas and he will not stop until he finds a serum that gets rid of the Godstrand once and for all.

Dr. Carl Julian/Praxagore

STR: 12	Action Points: 3
CON: 11	Damage Modifier: None
SIZ: 13	Power Points: 15
DEX: 12	Movement: 6 meters
INT: 17	Initiative Bonus: +15
POW: 14	Luck Points: 3
CHA: 13	Armor: None

Skills: Athletics 45%, Brawn 39%, Computers 52%, Deceit 72%, Electronics 54%, Endurance 45%, Evade 50%, Influence 64%, Insight 59%, Medicine 91%, Perception 60%, Pilot 42%, Research 76%, Science (Biology) 84%, Science (Chemistry) 79%, Science (Genetics) 88%, Stealth 47%, Streetwise 54%, System Ops 68%, Unarmed 47%, Willpower 70%

Passions: Extranormals must be eliminated 87%, Never forget my daughter 75%, Science solves any problem 67%

Gear: Smartphone, Celedrone caller

Hit Locations

1d20	Location	AP/HP
1-3	Right Leg	0/6
4-6	Left Leg	0/6
7-9	Abdomen	0/7
10-12	Chest	0/8
13-15	Right Arm	0/5
16-18	Left Arm	0/5
19-20	Head	0/6

Combat Style

Mad Scientist: 65%

Attacks

Attack	Size/Force	Range	Damage	AP/HP
Unarmed	S	-	1d3	-

When Dr. Julian uses his modified TALOS Unit as a battle suit, he gains the Damage Modifier, Abilities, and attacks as noted above for the Battle version. He also gains the Armor Value of the suit and increases his Hit Points by 2 in all Hit Locations. While in control of the robot, Dr. Julian uses all his normal Skill values as listed above, and his Initiative Bonus is reduced to +11.

Notes:

Street Level Praxagore: If you are using Street level Heroes, Dr. Julian's abilities remain the same and use the modifications listed for the TALOS Unit as listed above for the same Power Level but keep its Armor and Hit Point values as listed. It still uses Dr. Julian's Skill values for all checks.

Paragon Level Praxagore: If you are using Paragon level Heroes, Dr. Julian's abilities remain the same and use the modifications listed for the TALOS Unit as listed above for the same Power Level. It still uses Dr. Julian's Skill values for all checks, but the advanced targeting systems give him a +10% bonus to Combat Style and Unarmed rolls.

Callie Carter

Callie Carter moved to Gemelos City when she was just out of college, hoping to find a lucrative job at Phontonic Technologies in their software development department, but her timing unfortunately coincided with the company's decline. She took a series of IT support jobs and got sucked into the growing phenomenon of the Godstrand and the growing extranormal population in Gemelos City. She was fascinated by their abilities and how many of them were willing to risk their lives to help others, and she was frustrated by the growing legal restrictions placed on X-N activity. Using her computing expertise, she took up the role of activist, working to build communities of extranormals and their supporters and you build support resources for them. Soon, Callie noticed some of her X-N contacts going missing and she began to look into what was happening as a way of helping the people she had grown close to in the city.

Callie Carter

Action Points: 2
Damage Modifier: None
Power Points: 11
Movement: 6 meters
Initiative Bonus: +14
Armor: None
Abilities: None

Skills: Athletics 45%, Brawn 35%, Computers 72%, Drive 53%, Electronics 68%. Endurance 43%, Evade 51%, Influence 55%, Insight 61%, Perception 61%, Research 67%, Streetwise 62%, Unarmed 39%, Willpower 62%, Stealth 44%

Passions: Advocate for extranormals 67%, Stay off the grid 55%, Keep up with technology 60%

Gear: Smartphone, Laptop

Hit Locations

1d20	Location	AP/HP
1-3	Right Leg	0/5
4-6	Left Leg	0/5
7-9	Abdomen	0/6
10-12	Chest	0/7
13-15	Right Arm	0/4
16-18	Left Arm	0/4
19-20	Head	0/5

Combat Style

Intrepid Investigator: 40%

Attacks

Attack	Size/Force	Range	Damage	AP/HP
Unarmed	S	-	1d3	-

APPENDIX

The following are some random generator tables for use with this adventure or any *Destined* story you wish to tell. The first three are to help generate random Core Powers, Boosts, Limits, and Passions. A player can use them to randomly create all aspects of their hero or help inspire ideas during creation, and the Games Master can use them for Non-Player Characters and quick villains. There is also a table of random locations and events for a suburban area like the one included in this adventure to help the Games Master flesh out a location or serve as inspiration for an encounter.

RANDOM CORE POWERS TABLE

1d100	Core Power	Boosts	Limits
01-02	Adhesion	Boosts: *Expert Grappler, Sticky Fingers, Sudden Stop, Wallrunner*	Limits: *Limited Surfaces, Low Speed, Uncontrolled Stickiness*
03-05	Blast	Boosts: *Armor Piercing, Detonate, Ongoing Damage, Salvo*	Limits: *Inaccurate, Low Penetration, Short Range*
06-07	Close Combat Attack	Boosts: *Quick Draw, Ranged Parry, Toxic, Weapon Traits*	Limits: *Handheld, Poor Defense, Slow*
08-10	Combat Expert - Expertise: Archery, Bleeding Attack, Dual Weapon, Duelist, Grappling, Impaling Attack, Improvised, Longarm, Pinning Attack, Pistol, Reach, Throwing, Unarmed	Boosts: *Expert Strike, Precise Strike, Ready for Action, Speed Load*	Limits: *Signature Weapon, Weapon Focus, Weapon Wear*
11-12	Creation	Boosts: *Complex Objects, Distant Creations, Durable Creations, Large Creations*	Limits: *Fragile Creations, Limited Creations, Obvious Creations*
13-14	Deflect	Boosts: *Extra Parry, Fast Shield, Ranged Redirect, Tower Shield*	Limits: *Active Blocking, No Attack Option, One Attack Form*
15-16	Duplication	Boosts: *Additional Duplicate, Army of One, Human Target, Parallel Lives*	Limits: *Passionate Duplicates, Sympathetic Bond, Weak Duplicates*
17-18	Durability	Boosts: *Natural Detox, Second Wind, Shake It Off, Tireless*	Limits: *Crash, Glass Jaw, Lightweight*
19-20	Elemental Control	Boosts: *Create Element, Elemental Movement, Increased Area, Independent Element*	Limits: *Crude Shapes Only, Elemental Vulnerability, Willful Element*
21-22	Empathy	Boosts: *Emotion Control, Empathic Healing, Global Empathy, Read the Room*	Limits: *Empathic Mimic, Primal Empath, Specific Emotion*
23-24	Energy Field	Boosts: *Energy Flare, Energy Weapons, Fast Field, Selective Field*	Limits: *Always On, Destructive Field, Reactive Shield*
25-27	Enhanced Reactions	Boosts: *Additional Reactions, Nimble, Parkour, Superior Balance*	Limits: *Impulsive, On the Move, Overwhelmed*
28-29	Enhanced Speed	Boosts: *Hyper Action, Hyper Speed, Speed Charge, Whirlwind*	Limits: *Easily Winded, Hyper Metabolism, Jogger*
30-32	Enhanced Strength	Boosts: *Clobber, Ground Pound, Power Lift, Super Leap*	Limits: *Bull in a China Shop, Focused Strength, Muscle Strain*
-	Enhanced Strength Variant Power: Enhanced Body	-	-
33-34	Entrap	Boosts: *Guide Line, Strong Bindings, Swinging, Wide Net*	Limits: *Fragile Bindings, Single Location, Slowing Bindings*
35-36	Flight	Boosts: *Afterburners, Dive Bomb, Space Flight, Supersonic*	Limits: *Gliding, Levitate, Sky Rider*
-	Flight Variant Power: Super Swimming	Boosts: *Surface Launch*	Limits: *Aquatic*
37-38	Force Field	Boosts: *Bolster, Fire Point, Mobile Field, Shapeable Field*	Limits: *Limited Protection, Opaque, Weak Point*

Power Outage

Random Core Powers Table

1d100	Core Power	Boosts	Limits
39-40	Growth	Boosts: *Fast Change, Giant Escape, Swat, Titanic*	Limits: *Always On, Growth Strain, Slow Motion*
41-43	Heightened Sense - Senses: *Dark Sight, Echolocation, Enhanced Sense, Esoteric Sense, Night Vision, Vibration Sense*	Boosts: *Additional Sense, Telescopic Sense, Tracking Sense, X-Ray Sense*	Limits: *Overload, Sensory Static, Weakened Sense*
44-46	Inherent Armor	Boosts: *Armor Up, Human Shield, Nigh Invulnerability, Stand Fast*	Limits: *Ablative, Bulky, Partial Coverage*
-	Inherent Armor Variant Power: Material Mimic	Boosts: *Increased Duration, Thicker Armor*	-
47-48	Invisibility	Boosts: *Additional Senses, Afterimage, Shared Invisibility, Stealth Strike*	Limits: *Chameleon, Obvious Tell, Partial Invisibility*
49-50	Kinetic Control	Boosts: *Fast Charge, Kinetic Shield, Supercharge, Torpid Bubble*	Limits: *Body in Motion, Inaccurate Charge, Kinetic Drain*
51-53	Life Support - Conditions: *Intense Cold, Intense Heat, Intense Radiation, No Breathing, No Sleep, No Sustenance, Underwater, Vacuum*	Boosts: *Additional Environments, Environmental Adaptation, Limited Resistance, Survivalist*	Limits: *Limited Environment, Opposite Environment Susceptibility, Unusual Requirement*
-	Life Support Variant Power: Artificial Being	-	-
54-56	Lucky	Boosts: *Bad Penny, Environmental Editing, Luck of the Devil, Shared Luck*	Limits: *Black Cat, Fickle Fate, Karmic Backlash*
57-58	Morph	Boosts: *Doppelganger, Expert Shifter, Metamorph, Quick Change*	Limits: *Body Only, Persistent Flaw, Specific Form*
59-60	Negation	Boosts: *Additional Powers, Energy Drain, Power Thief, Ranged Negation*	Limits: *Backlash, Power Trade, Specific Power Origin*
61-62	Phantasm	Boosts: *Additional Senses, Greater Phantasm, Independent Illusion, Psychosomatic*	Limits: *Certain Senses Only, Psychic Illusion, Specific Phantasms*
63-65	Precognition	Boosts: *Danger Sense, Psychometry, Remote Viewing, Shared Fate*	Limits: *Cosmic Backlash, False Visions, Nightmares*
66-67	Regeneration	Boosts: *Back from the Dead, Instant Healing, Reptilian Regeneration, Shared Healing*	Limits: *Down for the Count, Single Location Only, Traumatic Regeneration*
68-70	Resistance	Boosts: *Absorption, Attack Redirection, Environmental Adaptation, Immunity*	Limits: *Damage Conversion, Linked Absorption, Living Bomb*
71-73	Savant	Boosts: *Instant Specialization, Jack of All Trades, Observational Memory, Parallel Knowledge*	Limits: *Educational Limits, Knowledge Gap, Skill Deficiency*
74-75	Sensory Overload	Boosts: *Additional Sense, Esoteric Senses, Flashbang, Increased Range*	Limits: *Feedback, Partial Sensory Loss, Quick Flash*
76-77	Shrinking	Boosts: *Growth Punch, Microscopic, Quick Shrink, Shrinking Dodge*	Limits: *Disorienting Shrinking, Growing Pains, Stressful Shrinking*
78-80	Stretching	Boosts: *Malleable, Maximum Stretch, Slingshot, Stretchy Evade*	Limits: *Rubbery, Slow Retraction, Weakened Limbs*
81-82	Summon	Boosts: *Empowered Construct, Guardian Constructs, Homunculus, Legion*	Limits: *Limited Form, Material Required, Sympathetic Link*
83-84	Technopathy	Boosts: *Data Transfer, Memory Probe, System Control, Wi-Fi Enabled*	Limits: *Direct Connection, Limited Access, System Short*
85-87	Telekinesis	Boosts: *Distance Manipulation, Size Matters Not, Telekinetic Shove, Telekinetic Strike*	Limits: *Limited Objects, Telekinetic Strain, Visible Force*
88-90	Telepathy	Boosts: *Gestalt Mind, Mind Control, Mind Probe, Party Line*	Limits: *Limited Access, Mental Overload, Oversharing*

Power Outage

Random Core Powers Table

1d100	Core Power	Boosts	Limits
91-93	Teleport	Boosts: *Full Stop, Long Jump, Quick Jump, Teleport Other*	Limits: *Conditional Jump, Dangerous Passage, Jump Disorientation*
-	Teleport Variant Power: Portals	Boosts: *Far Gate, Invisible Door, Persistent Portals*	Limits: *Inaccurate Portal*
94-95	Transform	Boosts: *Alchemy, Lasting Transformation, Ranged Transformation, Size Transformation*	Limits: *Limited Transformation, Unattended Objects, Unstable Transformation*
96-97	Vaporous Form	Boosts: *Non-Corporeal, Partial Manifestation, Quick Mist, Spectral Dodge*	Limits: *Dissipated Lungs, Grounded, Mist Vulnerability*
98-100	Choose any power	-	-

Random Hero Limits Table

1d100	Hero Limits
01-05	Activation Cost
06-09	Activation Time
10-14	Boosted Only
15-19	Concentration
20-23	Conditional
24-26	Distinctive Appearance
27-29	External Power Source*
30-34	Fatal Flaw*
35-39	Fatiguing
40-43	Impaired Recovery*
44-48	Latent
49-53	Limited Power
54-57	Limited Targets
58-63	Linked
64-68	Omnipower
69-73	Physical Limitation*
74-78	Poor Control
79-83	Power Outage
84-88	Powered Form*
89-92	Side Effect
93-96	Unstable Power
97-100	Vulnerability*

Random Passions Table

If you prefer a random approach to your character's inner mind, roll 1d100 for each random Passion you wish to generate in this way. Note: Some Passions listed here may be inherently incompatible with each other without some intense mental gymnastics.

1d100	Passion
01-05	The system is broken so I need to work outside it to serve justice.
06-10	My abilities represent a duty to protect those weaker than myself.
11-15	Knowledge is the greatest power.
16-20	My friends must never know about (my secret).
21-25	I owe my (mentor/organization) for helping me and I will do anything for them.
26-30	It is my sworn duty to protect (object/person/location/and so on).
31-35	(Paramour) is my one true love but I need to keep them away from my heroic persona to protect them.

Power Outage

RANDOM PASSIONS	
1d100	**Passion**
36-40	Those who do evil have no place in society and I will eliminate them.
41-45	Human life is sacred and I will never cause another's death.
46-50	There's nothing wrong with using my powers to make a little cash on the side.
51-55	The Law is the most important barrier between society and anarchy.
56-60	I will find the villain who killed my (loved one) and bring them to justice.
61-65	Animals are better companions than people.
66-70	I will make sure the people love me.
71-75	My (parent) was one of the first Heroes and I will do all I can to live up to their legacy.
76-80	There is nothing so serious that it cannot be joked about.
81-85	My services come with a price.
86-90	No one deserves cruelty.
91-95	Fear is my greatest weapon in my fight against injustice.
96-100	I will eliminate evil by any means available to me.

RANDOM SUBURB EVENTS/LOCATIONS TABLE	
1d100	**Location/Event**
01-05	Stellarharts Coffee: A gourmet coffee chain popular in Gemelos City and on the West Coast.
06-10	Public Park: A tranquil patch of nature in the middle of suburbia.
11-15	Restaurant: A fancy place with linen tablecloths or a fashionable eatery.
16-20	Garbage Day: Trash pickup is scheduled for the next day, so there are garbage cans out on the curbside in residential areas and large garbage trucks from early in the morning until early afternoon
21-25	Strip Mall: Populated with various shops and a restaurant or two.
26-30	Library: Shhhh! Come for the books, stay for the free computer access.
31-35	Fast Food Restaurant: Quick service chain eatery with reasonable prices.
36-40	Clothing Store: Either a chain retail store or a local boutique.
41-45	Big Box Store: A large chain retailer that has just about anything you need at low, low prices.
46-50	Construction Site: Coming soon, a new business, office, or house.
51-55	Grocery Store: A chain store or a local place well stocked with good things to eat.
56-60	Stellarharts Coffee: Come grab an Oki gohan latte!
61-65	Convenience Store: Quick stop for snacks, gas, or scratch off lottery tickets.
66-70	Auto Repair: A chain repair store that specializes in oil changes and new tires or a local garage with appropriately grizzled mechanics.
71-75	Damien Diablo: Attorney-at-Law: He will fight for you to Hell and back.
76-80	Bits and Dongles: Computer parts and accessories.
81-85	Farmer's Market: Try the honey crisp apples!
86-90	Another Stellarharts Coffee: They breed like rabbits.
91-95	Permian Petroleum: Fill 'er up.
96-100	Extranormal Response Unit: A squad of officers in tactical gear responding to reports of X-N activity.

Maps and Plans

Power Outage

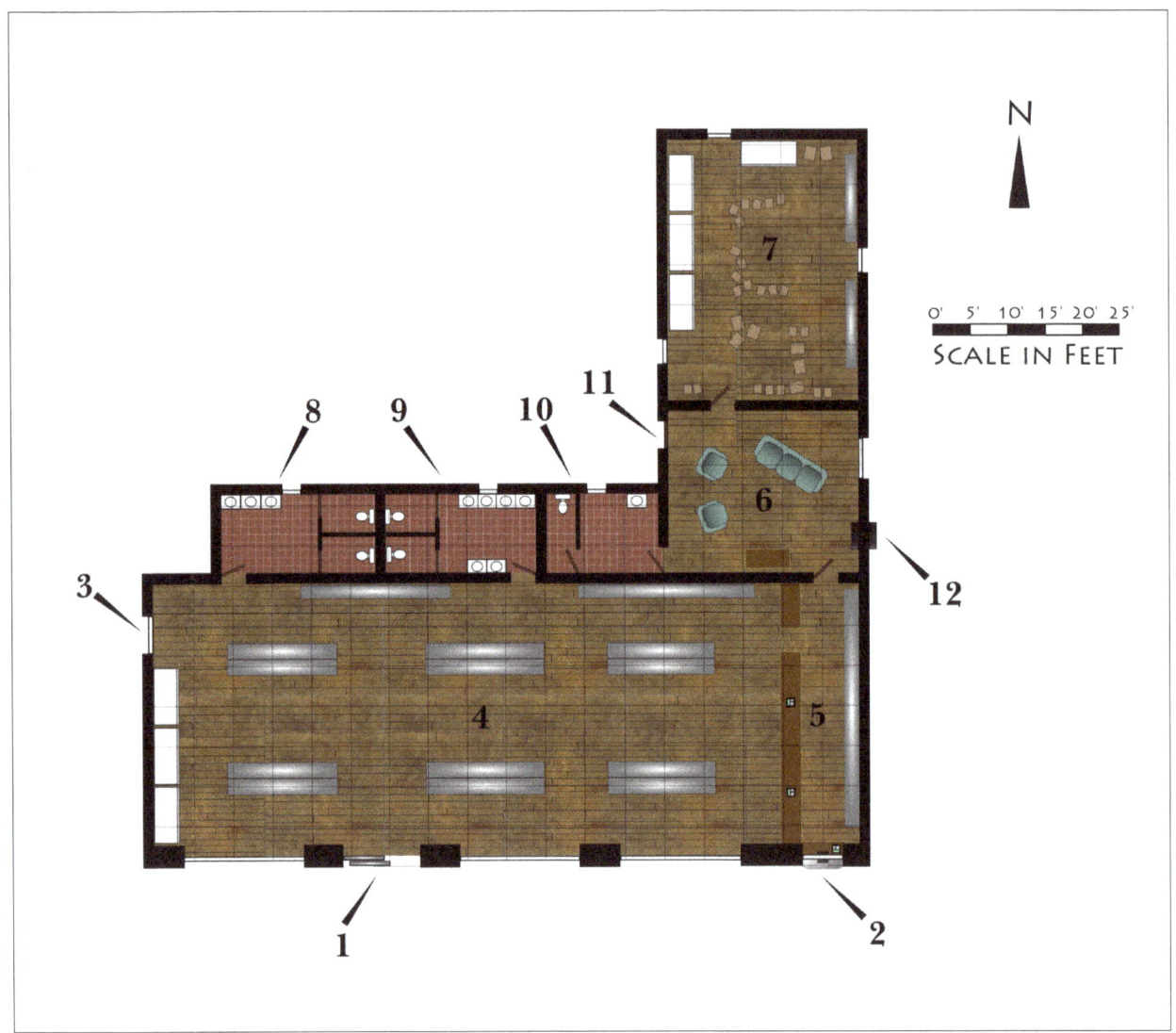

The Convenience Store

Key

1. Front Door
2. Service Window
3. Fire Exit
4. Shop Floor
5. Counter & Tills
6. Staff Break Room
7. Store Room
8. Men's Customer Restroom
9. Women's Customer Restroom
10. Staff Restroom
11. Back Door
12. Emergency Fuel Supply Cut-off Valves (internal & external)

Power Outage

The Convenience Store and Environs

Key

1. Gas Pumps under Canopy
2. The Store
3. Slip-roads to Gemelos Highway
4. Grass Verge between Highway and Gas Station Forecourt

Power Outage

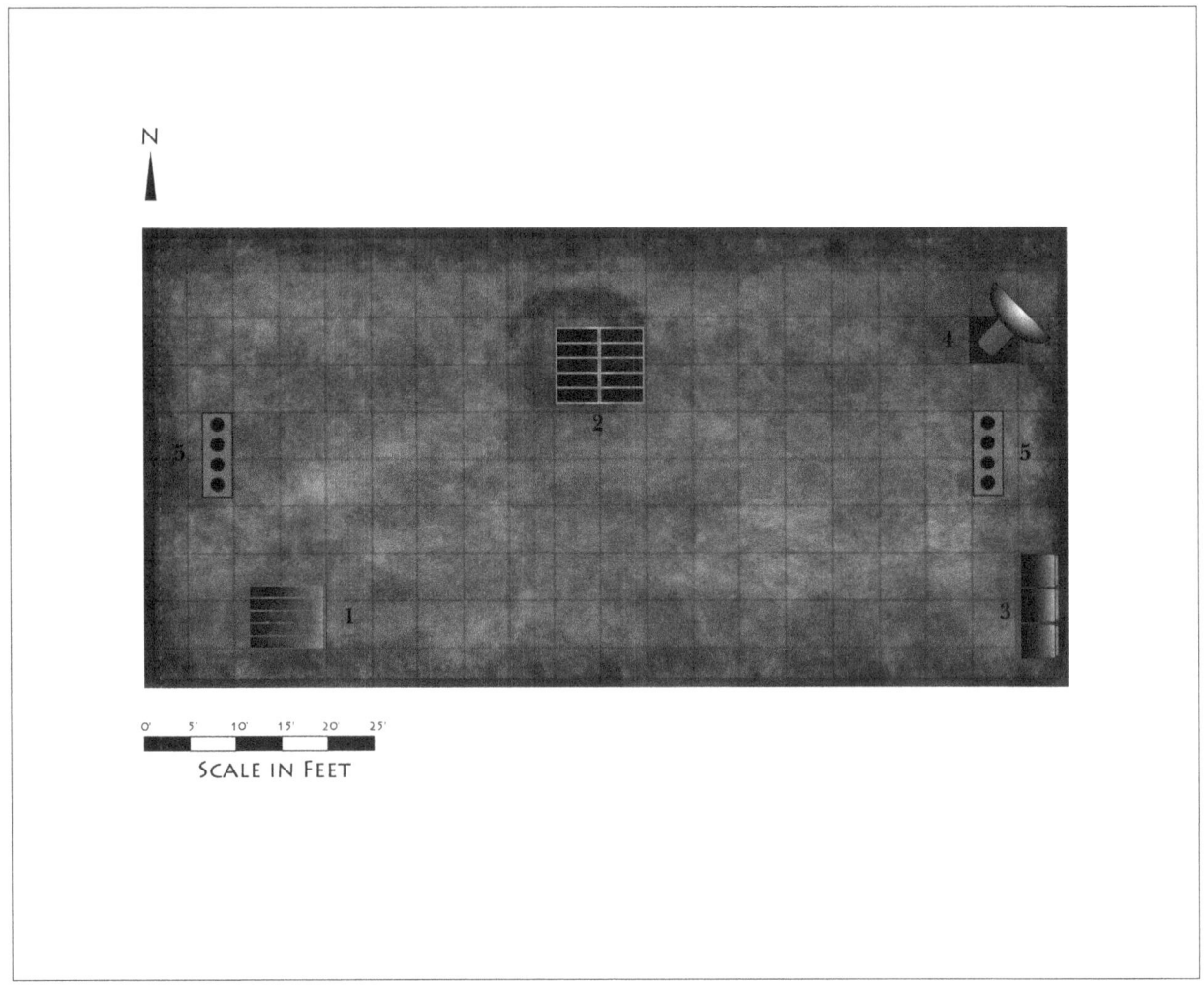

The Clinic Roof

Key

1. Stairs up from interior
2. Skylight (one storey drop to offices below)
3. Air-conditioning Plant
4. Satellite Dish
5. Chimney stacks

Power Outage

The Convenience Store and Environs: Players' Map

Power Outage

The Clinic Roof: Players' Map

Milton Keynes UK
Ingram Content Group UK Ltd.
UKHW050203241124
451541UK00008B/61